IN SERVICE *to* SPIRIT

RICHARD LANIGAN

In Service to Spirit

tellwell

Tellwell Talent
www.tellwell.ca

ISBN
978-0-2288-6250-5 (Paperback)
978-0-2288-6251-2 (eBook)

TABLE OF CONTENTS

Acknowledgements v
Foreword ix

CHAPTER 1 – The Beginning 1
CHAPTER 2 – That Knowing Feeling 5
CHAPTER 3 – Life Changes Forever 9
CHAPTER 4 – Spiritual Teachings Begin 11
CHAPTER 5 – Amazing Proof from Spirit 16
CHAPTER 6 – Back to the Future 20
CHAPTER 7 – Spirit Heals My Son 22
CHAPTER 8 – My Mother's Passing 24
CHAPTER 9 – Joining a Spiritualist Church 27
CHAPTER 10 – Meeting Silver Birch 30
CHAPTER 11 – My Learning Continues 34
CHAPTER 12 – My First Mediumship Readings 38
CHAPTER 13 – Life-Altering Experience 41
CHAPTER 14 – Opening St. Brigid's Spiritual Centre 44
CHAPTER 15 – Moving Forward 47
CHAPTER 16 – My Sacred Place 50
CHAPTER 17 – A Most Beautiful Gift from Spirit 55
CHAPTER 18 – One Door Closes, Another Opens 60
CHAPTER 19 – Spiritual Healings 63
CHAPTER 20 – Amazing Revelations 69
CHAPTER 21 – Silver Birch 73
CHAPTER 22 – Spirit Reveals My Mission 76

ACKNOWLEDGEMENTS

I wish to sincerely thank the following people who have helped me along my spiritual journey. My wife Barbara Lanigan, who has supported me from day one even though she did not entirely believe in what I was doing until she had her own special experiences with Spirit. Thank you for your love and exceptional support. Sharon Ames, who taught me some amazing spiritual lessons that have yielded phenomenal experience and joy for me. Janice Dodds, who has supported me from day one and was there on the opening day of our spiritual centre even though she was unwell at the time. Patricia Strong, who came into my life just at the right time and together we turned our centre into St. Brigid's Spiritualist Church. We had four amazing years working and building the church together and have forged a lifelong friendship. Jill Washington, Kim Degner Taylor, and Bobbie Pineau are three beautiful ladies who joined our church under different circumstances and are all now ordained ministers, certified spiritual mediums and healers and, along with myself, take care of all the ministerial duties of our church. Nancy Lanigan has served on our Board of Directors since our church opened and Dana Tate is another wonderful lady who has served on our board for many years along with our most recent board members, Katrina Blumhagen and Debbie Pineo. The rest of our board members are the four ministers. All of these wonderful people are the engine that keeps our church going and I sincerely thank each and every one of them for their outstanding service to Spirit. A huge thank you to Shelley Youell for creating the beautiful cover for my book.

Shelley is a wonderful spiritual medium and psychic artist and it is an honour to have her spiritual input in my book.

Blessings,
Richard Lanigan

I live with my partner, Shawn, and our three cuddly dogs. I am a mother of three, and a proud grandma of two beautiful grandchildren. I was born in Toronto, Ontario and raised in Edmonton, Alberta. I grew up in a home where it was normal for the women in the family to sit around the kitchen table reading tarot cards, interpreting tea leaves, and connecting with the spirit world. My understanding of the spirit world began when I met Reverend Richard Lanigan at St. Brigid's Spiritualist Church of Edmonton. There I learned about spirit communication and spiritual healing. I eventually became an ordained spiritualist minister through the Spiritualist Church of Canada. I am now one of the ministers at St. Brigid's Spiritualist Church. I believe spiritual growth and guidance is there for all those who desire it. You can contact Rev. Jill Washington through our website at www.stbrigidsspiritualistchurch.ca.

Jill Washington,

I am a married mom of three beautiful kids and two small dogs and a cat. I was born in Hinton, Alberta and moved to the Edmonton area to go to post-secondary to become a Paralegal. By day I am a Paralegal. At night I spend time with my family, sit in weekly circle, and do other church related activities. I was ordained by the Spiritualist Church of Canada in October 2019, and my home church is St. Brigid's. I grew up in a family that did not practice religion, but I always knew there was something bigger. After three close people in my life died tragically and young within a year, I found myself wanting to learn more about communicating with the other side. I found Rev. Lanigan and he has mentored me in my beautiful journey. I love sharing Spirit with others and my favorite feeling is when I see the tears of healing that come with a meaningful message from Spirit.

Kim Taylor,

I am married to my best friend and biggest support. We have four grown children and three grandsons as well as two crazy yorkies. I was born and raised in the Okanagan region of British Columbia and moved to Alberta to attend University/College.

While living in central Alberta I developed my relationship with Spiritualism at the Calgary First Spiritualist Church. Always intuitive and spiritual, I never had a place that felt like I belonged. Thankfully when I was introduced to Spiritualism, it felt like home. I spent years building a rapport with the Spirit World and learning to trust in the communication, taking every opportunity to learn and develop. I started beginner Mediumship classes at different Churches in Alberta and then furthered my learning by taking courses with Tutors from the UK and attending the prestigious Arthur Findlay College in England several times. I also took classes in Spiritual Healing and gained a passion for that as well.

It was my work in the IT department of a school division that brought me to Edmonton, where I met Rev. Richard Lanigan and became a part of St. Brigid's Spiritualist Church. I had been sad to leave my community at the Spiritualist Church in Calgary but leaving there brought me the blessing that Rev. Richard and St. Brigid's are to me. In April of 2020, with the support of Richard, I was ordained by the Spiritualist Church of Canada.

I believe that being in service to the Spirit World is a calling and I feel honored to be able to work on their behalf to bring healing and comfort from their world to ours.

Love and hugs,
Bobbi Pineau,

FOREWORD

This is the story of my life but what I want to focus on is the beautiful and amazing spiritual events that I have experienced. I am talking about the most powerful, divine force in the universe which is known as God, or Creator, or the Infinite Intelligence to name a few, or whatever it is that you call the God of your understanding. This power is around and about every living thing in the universe. All human beings, every animal, mammal, bird, and all living organisms. This is so because this Supreme Being created the universe and everything in it and because of this, all human beings have a piece of this divine power within each of us. This divine power is our own spirit which is the real you, and when the life of our earth bodies comes to an end our spirit returns to the spirit world which is our real home. It is the relationship with the spirit world and those that reside there that this true story is about and my intention in sharing this with the reader is to hopefully help them to realise that this great divine power is available to everyone in the world; all you have to do is to acknowledge Spirit and ask for it to be part of your life and then build a strong and beautiful relationship with it.

July 30, 2020

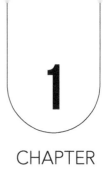

1
CHAPTER

THE BEGINNING

I was born on March 29, 1952 at 41 Kilkenny Street, Castlecomer in County Kilkenny, Ireland. This was my grandparents' home on my mother's side of the family. My parents lived in Dublin in a rather crowded place so my mother went back to her parents' place to give birth to her first three children. My mother delivered all of her children at home with a midwife in attendance. After I was born my parents got their own home in Dublin and my other five siblings were born there at 3 Glenside Villas, Palmerstown, Dublin 20, Ireland. There were eight children altogether, with five boys and three girls. Our parents were Christopher and Elizabeth Lanigan.

I came into the world at exactly 6 p.m. My mom was delighted with this because she was of the Catholic faith and every day at noon and 6 p.m. the churches would ring the bells and this was known as the bells of the Angelus, which is a call to prayer and to spread goodwill to everyone. An even more exciting part of my birth was that I was an en caul birth, or veiled birth. This rare birth happens in less than one in 80,000 births. It is believed that this baby is very spiritual and will possess the gift of healing by the laying on of hands. It is also believed that such a person can never die by drowning and so back in the day sailors would purchase a small piece of the dried caul to carry with them when they went to sea in the belief that it would keep them safe. When I was about four years old spirit began to work with me. I don't remember much about that time as I was very young and it did not mean anything to me. My mother told me that I would be playing with my toys when suddenly I would stop playing and I would go to her and start telling her a story. At first my mum did not understand what I meant, as when I finished telling her whatever I had to say I would just go back to playing with my toys again as if nothing had happened. After this happened a few times, my mum realised that the things I would tell her would actually take place a short while after. This is what is known as a premonition. So Spirit was telling me about things that would happen in the near future. Now this was very exciting but it was 1956 in Ireland which was a predominantly Catholic country and this sort of thing would be seen as the work of the devil. My mum told me to keep this as our secret, just between her and me. This of course was her way of protecting me and our family from public ridicule and scorn. My father died never knowing anything about this because he would never have condoned it.

Another amazing thing that happened between the age of four and five was that I astral travelled. It suddenly began one night after I went to sleep and abruptly ended three months later. Although I was very young when this occurred, I vividly remember it all because I did not understand it and at the end of each astral travel I would wake up screaming with fright. After successive nights of this happening, my parents would put me to bed and watch me fall asleep. They would sit on either side of my bed and be there to comfort me when I would wake up screaming and frightened. This usually happened three times every night and then I would settle down and sleep comfortably for the rest of the night. My poor parents were frantic for answers and the doctors did not have anything of substance to offer them. They genuinely thought that there was something mentally wrong with me and then my astral travelling suddenly stopped and it never happened again. It was a fascinating experience even though it was frightful for a young child and I will explain it for you to the best of my ability. The amazing thing was that I was able to watch my spirit leave my body and return to it again after my travels. It was like I was sitting opposite myself and my forehead would open up where our third eye is located and I would be standing there. I was all of maybe two inches tall and I would look out to my left to see if there was anything coming. As I recall there was never anything coming so I would jump out and always to my right. As soon as I jumped out I found that I was flying and that I was on some type of a circular track, and the other thing was once I was out I always felt that I was being chased. I could not see who or what was chasing me but I always had the uncomfortable feeling that whatever it was they were just about to catch me. The opening in my forehead looked like the mouth of a cave and so I remember I would speed up and head towards it because I knew that once I got inside this cave I would be safe. And I instinctively knew that whatever was chasing me was not allowed to follow me into the cave. Sometimes as I was heading to my cave I would feel that I could not slow down to make my entrance because my pursuers would then catch me, instead I would speed up even faster and race around the track to gain more distance between me and them. This always worked and I was never caught. However, the problem was that I would come crashing back into my body instead of gently re-entering it slowly and that is why I would wake up screaming and frightened. Later in life I realised that my spirit would leave my body and go to the spirit world to play with the spirit children and that is what my astral travelling was all about. At that time, there was nothing to fear about it but I did not understand it and so it was fear of the unknown. The spirit children were simply playing tag with me. When I reached about eight years old I discovered my mum had shared our secret with three of her closest girlfriends. These women were a few years younger than my mum and all married and beginning to start their own families. What transpired was that as each of these ladies became pregnant they would visit my mum and ask me to predict the sex of their babies, as there was no ultrasound available at that time. I would play along and I was never wrong in predicting the sex of the babies. When one of these ladies was pregnant with her third child she was convinced that this time I was wrong because she felt this pregnancy was different from her other ones, but it turned out I was right again. They asked me how I did this and I said that I did not know but that I had this knowing feeling of whether the baby was a boy or girl.

2

CHAPTER

THAT KNOWING FEELING

I remember when I was ten years old I got this realization that there was no fear in dying. It was something that just came to me and again I knew it was right but I had nothing to prove it. I distinctly remember being concerned for all my brothers and sisters, my parents, my grandparents, aunts and uncles, and all family members. My concern for them was that they may be afraid of dying and I wanted to protect them but I did not know how. Since that day I have never been afraid of dying, which has given me a huge sense of freedom and relaxation about the whole subject. As I approached my teenage years I had this feeling that I was different from other kids. I was not sure how but again I had this knowing that I was different but I could not put my finger on it. Sometimes my friends would say I was weird, usually after I would tell them not to trespass on some farmer's property because they would get caught. I would not go with them and sure enough they would get caught. They would ask me how I knew they would get caught and all I could tell them was that I had a feeling about it. Life was a little lonely at times because people did not understand me and I did not understand the things I knew and felt. I was never sad about any of it and my lonely times were actually very happy times that I spent alone trying to figure out how I was different and trying to understand it all. I had this great relationship with my Nana Lanigan and she lived very close to us so I could just walk up the road a couple of hundred yards and I was at her place. Many days after school I would go there and hang out with her. She raised chickens and some turkeys and she let me feed them with her and collect the chicken eggs. When she had chickens that she harvested for food I would sit with her and pluck the feathers by hand to get them ready for cooking. Many times she would give my dad a chicken and lots of fresh eggs to help feed our large family. She had apple trees and fruit berry bushes which she generously shared with our family. My mum would then bake apple pies and make jam from these wholesome products. There was a road at the back of Nana Lanigan's house that led down into a valley where two rivers ran through our town. On Sunday afternoons, weather permitting, we often went for a walk down this road and along the river banks. It was beautiful down there and was also the place where I learned to fish. It would turn out to be a very important place in my life and my favourite place to be.

When I was about eleven years old my parents allowed me to go fishing on my own. I would go down to the rivers most days after school and many days I would catch enough fish to feed the whole family. As I became more comfortable and familiar with my surroundings down by the rivers I began to venture further away from our village, staying alongside the rivers so that I would not get lost. As I ventured further, I came across a wooded area and the rivers ran right through it. As I approached this forest there was an old wooden door with an ancient iron latch and keyhole. Fortunately the door was not locked and I could open it with the latch and gain entry into the forest. I closed the door behind me and it was like I had just entered another world. As I walked through the forest with a river running on each side of me, the birds were chirping and every now and then the sun would break through an opening in the treetops. The forest was maybe a half-mile long in total but as I came to the end of it I began to hear a familiar noise and as I turned around the last bend there was this majestic waterfall flowing in all of its beauty. This truly was and still is an enchanted forest. This forest became my favourite place to go and many times when my friends declined to go there, I would go alone. It was at these times that I would get the feeling that I was not alone. I had a strong feeling that someone was watching me and it made me slightly uneasy but it never deterred me from going there. Later in life I would discover that this was my spirit guide who is my constant companion that I could feel with me and he was walking my path with me and looking out for me and keeping me safe when I was alone in a forest with two rivers close by. I spent the best part of six years in this magical place and it was a huge part of my amazing and very happy childhood. At fifteen years of age I was heavily involved in sports and loved every minute of it. I was playing hurling, which is Ireland's national game, and Gaelic football for our local club and also for our school. I later added soccer to my activities, so between games and practice I did not have much time for anything else. It was also time to start thinking about my future. I always wanted to be a motor mechanic but growing up in Ireland in the sixties the pickings were slim and I, like my older brother and sister, was expected to start working and contributing to the expense of our large family. I worked at some odd jobs until a chance came up with my dad's sister, my aunt Eileen and her business partner. They had a carpet installation company and so I started my apprenticeship with them to be a carpet installer on January 27, 1968. A few months before that I met and started dating a girl who would turn out to be my future wife. At the time of writing, Barbara and I have been together for fifty-three years. We have three wonderful sons and, so far, three beautiful grandchildren. We have walked a long, interesting and amazing path together; we have had our ups and downs, our good times and tough times, but we would not change any of it for anything. We were married on June 11, 1974 and we emigrated and arrived in Canada on May 27, 1975. We settled down in Edmonton, Alberta and I remember feeling a new sense of freedom. The main reason for that was in this big, beautiful land there were many different people from countries all over the world living here and as a result there was a great freedom to believe and practice what your religious beliefs are. I had not told my wife about the psychic experiences in my life but that was all about to change. I began to share my early experiences with her but she did not believe in that sort of thing. In the summer of 1976 Barbara suffered a miscarriage and we lost our first baby, but in November 1977 we welcomed our first son, Mark, into the family. On April 21-1980 our second son, Declan, arrived. Life was good and we were a very excited and happy family.

3

CHAPTER

LIFE CHANGES FOREVER

On July 8, 1980 my dad suddenly died. His death devastated me as I had not seen him for a couple of years and now I would never see him again. To make matters worse, I could not get home for my dad's funeral. The day before his passing we bought our first home and I literally did not have the money to fly home and also be out of work, and because I needed to fly immediately the airlines wanted three times the regular cost of a ticket. I was in an impossible situation, and so I missed attending my dad's funeral. This constantly played on my mind. Three months after my dad's passing, my wife told me she had something to tell me and that I needed to listen to her. She proceeded to tell me that the night after my dad died he appeared to her. I was asleep and it was about 2:00 a.m. She had gotten up and went downstairs to prepare a bottle to feed our new baby, Declan. She came back up and was in the baby room feeding him when my dad appeared to her and said, "Please look after Richard, you know how he is." My dad was referring to how his death was affecting me and also the fact that I suffered from nervousness and severe panic attacks. Barbara is a much calmer person than I and she knew me very well and so Dad trusted her to take care of me. I should have been delighted that my dad came to visit Barbara but after all I knew she did not believe in this kind of phenomena. So I questioned my wife about it and I suggested that she had dreamt it but she insisted that she was totally awake and reminded me that she had been downstairs to make the baby's bottle and was in the process of feeding him when my dad appeared and spoke to her. Barbara described how my dad was dressed and when I mentioned this to my mum a short time later she confirmed that Barbara saw my dad in the clothes he was buried in. This was a game changer for me and it would change my life forever. I was worried that my mum could pass quickly and at any time, so I sold up our house and holiday trailer and we returned home to Ireland. I did settle down back home but after about a year I realised I could not bring my dad back and I also realised that I and my wife and children had a much better life in Canada. So after sixteen months we returned to Canada but I decided to live in beautiful Victoria, British Columbia because I love the ocean and I dearly missed it. We lasted another sixteen months in Victoria, but I found the economy there was not good for a tradesman to raise a family and from experience I knew Edmonton Alberta would be much better for us economically. All the signs were pointing to Edmonton as if it was my destiny.

4

CHAPTER

SPIRITUAL TEACHINGS BEGIN

On May 10, 1985 our third son, Richard, was born. Later in life he would play a vital role in my development as a spiritual healer. It took my dad twenty years to come back to visit me. It was the summer of 2000 and one night when I went to bed he made his appearance. I like to sleep in a completely dark room and as I closed my eyes there was this very bright light and it startled me. My first thought was that my wife had turned the light on. I opened my eyes to find the room was completely dark. As soon as I reclosed my eyes this brilliant light was there again. I opened my eyes again because my next thought was that my neighbour had turned on his patio lights, which are right beside my bedroom window. When I opened my eyes to check this out my room was completely dark. I could not figure out what was going on and when I closed my eyes again this brilliant light appeared once more and this time I kept my eyes closed. I watched in awe as the light grew into a beautiful circle and there in the middle of it stood my dad. He just smiled at me and he did not say anything but I had the feeling that something else was to come from this.

I got my answer about a week later. I had gone to bed early as I was to play in a golf tournament the following morning and I had an early tee time. I was soon fast asleep but I was awakened at exactly 10 p.m., and I saw my dad in this light again and he had his arms wrapped around someone and they were literally jumping joyously together. My dad kept saying, "I have him, I have him," and then everything stopped and they were gone. I knew I had just witnessed my dad meeting someone who had just crossed over. When I got up the next morning my wife said that it was a beautiful sunny day and a great day for golf. I told my wife that someone in the family had died last night and I was feeling down. I related the experience I had with my dad and told her I could not make out who the person was with my dad. My wife told me to forget it and to go and enjoy my day. Well, the following day being Monday I was still very bothered so I called my mum in Ireland to inquire about the family and before I could say anything she said I have some bad news for you. She told me that my uncle Jim had passed away on Sunday morning at 5 a.m. Now, that time was important because it would be 10 p.m. on Saturday night where I lived in Canada. So I was privileged to see my father meet and receive his brother at the moment of his passing. The other significant thing was that when I saw my uncle Jim with my dad he had all of his limbs but my uncle had one of his legs amputated a few years prior to his passing. He was now complete again.

In the early fall of 1991 I was installing carpet in a house when a voice started talking to me in my head. It kept repeating one small sentence over and over, which was: "You have to get back to your spirituality." I could hear this very clearly but I just ignored it because I did not understand it. You see, growing up in a Catholic environment we did not use the term spirituality so it meant nothing to me. Well, this was spirit speaking to me and they were not going to take no for an answer. This sentence was repeated over and over for at least ten minutes and it became very annoying until finally out of total frustration I shouted, "Okay." As soon as I accepted the message, the sentence stopped being said. I arrived home that evening about seven and when I entered my home Spirit took over again. I walked into our home and immediately said to my wife that I needed to go out into the back yard and that she should just leave me alone there for a while. I had no idea what I was going to do out there as I was basically being led to do this. It was a beautiful fall evening with a completely clear sky and I was compelled to just gaze at the splendour of the night sky with the bright full moon and the sparkling stars and the planets that were in view at that time of year. It was an awe-inspiring spectacle and I realised that Spirit wanted me to appreciate the beauty and amazement of creation. I gazed at the beautiful night sky for about half an hour and I recall it as one of the most satisfying and comforting moments of my life. I went back inside and explained to my wife what had happened. This event inspired me to want to know more about spirituality as Spirit had insisted me to accept. I went to a bookstore to see what I could find on the subject but I was totally drawn to books about the afterlife. I finally settled on a book about a lady who died on the operating table but was revived after four minutes. The book was about where she went and what she saw. I was fascinated and totally hooked. I was buying and reading at least one book every week on the subjects of death and dying and the afterlife. I had an insatiable appetite for knowledge and I read over two hundred booked over the next three years. I was now learning a lot about psychics and mediums and spirit communication and it was fascinating information. I had not found any teachers for this in the Edmonton area, so I was educating myself in the best way that I could. I was trying to understand the phenomena associated with spiritualism and I realised that Spirit had been contacting me for most of my life. The things I used to hear in my head when I was young and now later in life as well. Also the way that I would just know things that were true or were going to happen were promptings from Spirit. I had lots of good information now on Spirit and the spirit world but I needed more so I decided to try and do journaling. I had read somewhere that people did this but I did not understand what it was really for. I mistook journaling for what is known as inspirational writing. This is where a medium would sit and connect with Spirit and write down what they would receive from Spirit. At this point in my life I did not even know how to meditate so I found myself a quiet place in our home and I sat with a journal and pen and I made myself be as calm and quiet as I could. I dated the page and sat ready for about a half hour. Nothing happened and I noted this on the page. I waited a few months and tried again and this time it was amazing what happened. Spirit dictated a full page of information to me and ended by saying that this was my lesson for today. I would sit with Spirit every few months and receive information which would be a new lesson for me. Every now and then I look back on these lessons and as time goes by they have even more meaning to me because I have learned and experienced so much more from Spirit that I have seen the meaning of those lesson become fulfilled. They are a real treasure to me.

Another wonderful gift that Spirit shared with me was they would wake me up at night, usually after midnight, and they would dictate information to me. The first time this happened I could hear a most beautiful poem or song about life. It was so beautiful I lay there enjoying it and I remember telling myself that I would write it down the next morning. Well of course when I awoke in the morning I could not remember a single word. I decided to keep a pen and paper by my bedside and sure enough a short time later I was awakened by Spirit and they started dictating to me right away. They first gave me the title of the piece which is 'The Essence of a Father.' I wrote everything down as fast as I could and after they were finished dictating this to me, which took about four minutes, I put it away and the next day I literally had to decipher what I had scribbled down. It turned out to be a beautiful piece and I had it typed up and printed. A short time later the same thing happened after midnight again and the title of this one is 'Serenity.' It is a very beautiful piece about what a mother is. I had this one dated and typed and printed. On several occasions on Father's Day and Mother's Day I would give a copy of these to the congregants of our spiritual church. Spirit did this a third time and I dutifully wrote everything down. Unfortunately I put this one aside for some reason and never did get around to getting it printed. That proved to be the end of Spirit working with me in that way. It was a dear lesson for me to learn. You see, when Spirit shares something with you and you don't follow through with it they will stop because Spirit will never force you to do anything. They will share some magic with you but we as humans have free will to accept or decline on anything. I still have the writing from that night and I do intend to get it printed and share it and maybe Spirit will take up this pursuit with me again. I believe they would, especially if I declare that I would like to participate in this again.

5

CHAPTER

AMAZING PROOF FROM SPIRIT

One Friday night when we arrived home after an evening out with some friends, I had a most amazing visit from Spirit. I want to point out that I never have and never will attempt to do any spiritual work when I have consumed alcohol, and I had on this occasion. I have since discovered that if Spirit needs you for something that just can't wait, they will come to you whether you like it or not, and on this occasion it turned out to be an emergency. This is what happened. It was around midnight and I felt a little hungry so I told my wife that I was going to heat up a baked potato that was left over from dinner. My wife went to bed and I put the potato in the microwave to heat it. When it was ready, I took it out and began to cut it into slices and then this extremely clear voice started to speak to me inside my head, and the following is exactly what happened. It was a female voice and it said: "Now you would like some butter with your potato." Now I like to eat my baked potatoes dry, absolutely nothing on them as I really like the dry fluffy texture, so I answered back and said no. The voice again said, "You really would like some butter on your potato." Well, I had learned from the past not to argue with Spirit. I got some butter and put it on the potato and ate it and when I did the voice stopped speaking. As soon as I finished eating, the conversation began again, and the voice said, "Now didn't you enjoy that?" I replied, "Yes, I did," and the Spirit said, "Do you remember when you were younger and you used to visit me on your summer holidays?" We would harvest the new small potatoes and we would boil a large pot of them and have them for dinner. The family would sit around the dining room table and eat the potatoes and just put butter on them. I do remember them being delicious. I now knew who the spirit was that was with me. It was my Nana Brennan, who was my mother's mom. She went to all that trouble to prove to me who she was because if she had just come to me and said who she was I most likely would not have believed her. She then said that I was to phone my mum because she was very distressed. I said no because it was seven in the morning in Ireland and it was too early to wake up my mum. Now Spirit does not get angry with us or shout at us in order to get us to comply with them, but when my Nana told me for a second time it was like my whole body felt her words and I knew I had to call my mum. I immediately called my mum's number and she answered the phone on its first ring. I said, "Hello Mum," and she said, "Oh, Richard! It would be you that would call me." I asked what was the matter she replied that she was home alone and that there was a burglar in her house. Mum's home was a two-storey house and she was upstairs in her bedroom and she could hear the burglar downstairs. Well, that moment terrified me as I did not know what would happen next. Would I hear my mother being attacked, or worse? And I was six thousand miles away in my home in Canada, and feeling helpless. I had a separate phone line in my house for business and so I told my mum that I would have my wife Barbara stay on the phone with her and I would use my business phone to call one of my brothers who lived very close by to mum and get them and the police to go to her house right away. My mum was so scared that she begged me to stay on the phone with her. As I was trying to convince her that it was best that I get help to her she suddenly said that she could hear the intruder leaving her house through a window downstairs. My mum knew her house very well as she had already lived there for over fifty years and she knew exactly how and where the burglar entered and exited her home. As I chatted with Mum about what had happened, we decided that when the burglar heard the phone being answered after only one ring they thought that someone was up from bed and they ran away before they were caught. I then told my mum how her mother had come to tell me to call her because you were very distressed. I reminded my mum that her mother was still caring for her and that she is never alone.

It was an amazing experience for me and I was left with no doubt that we do survive death on Earth and we simply go back to our real home in the spirit world. The communication from my Nana Brennan was so clear and was so accurate that I realised I was not crazy for hearing voices in my head but that spirit communication was real and I was privileged to be a part of it. On December 19, 1995 I received another wonderful visit from Spirit, but this time in a different way. Our three sons had all gone to friends for sleepovers and my wife and I were home alone. I went to bed early to read and my wife watched television in our living room. After about an hour my wife joined me in bed as she wanted company and she turned on the television in our bedroom. I was a little annoyed as I was enjoying reading my book in the quietness of our bedroom. A short time later my wife fell asleep on my shoulder so I took the remote control and turned off the television. I did not disturb her as she was asleep on my shoulder and we were both comfortable. All was quiet when suddenly a clear male voice from outside the bedroom door said, "Hello." It was loud enough to waken my wife and she raised her head up and said, "What was that?" I asked her what she had heard and she immediately answered that someone had said hello. I agreed that I heard the same thing. We both got out of bed to investigate because our youngest son Richard was famous for never staying the full night whenever he would go to someone's place for a sleepover. We checked the other bedrooms and all rooms in the house but there was nobody at home except my wife and I. We got back into bed and I was racking my brain trying to think who this might have been because the voice felt familiar to me. I had the feeling that today was important and I asked my wife what today's date was and she said it was December nineteenth. I excitedly told my wife that this was my dad's birthday. This was wonderful as both of us clearly heard his voice, as Dad came to say hello. This was the best Christmas present ever. Thanks, Dad.

6

CHAPTER

BACK TO THE FUTURE

Does the future already exist? Well, from one incredible experience I had with Spirit my conclusion is that yes, the future does already exist. I am always open and excited to learn more about spiritualism, the spirit world, and the amazing phenomena associated with it all but until I get a more valid explanation of the event that I am now going to share with you I shall abide by my decision that the future already exists. From my studies of Spirit I have learned that time does not exist in the spirit world and that the past, present, and future are all in the same realm and that, as spirits, we can visit any one of these areas at any time we want to.

The event I want to share here happened one evening when I was playing a game of soccer. It was an important game as it was the semi-final of a cup competition and the winner would go on to play in the final and the loser would be eliminated. The game was very competitive and was tied at half-time with neither team scoring. The team I played for was called Shamrock Rovers; I was the captain and I played in a midfield position. Not long after the second half started, this huge screen appeared in the sky and it was like I was pulled into it and my team and the soccer field that we were playing on all disappeared and I was now watching the same game with the same teams on the same field on this huge screen in the sky. I watched as one of my team players took a shot on the opposing goal and the ball went wide. The goalkeeper retrieved the ball and kicked it back into play. As I was playing the midfield, the ball was kicked to the far left of me and was going out of play at the sideline when one of the opposing players jumped up and headed the ball down to keep it in play. The ball landed directly in front of me, bounced once on the field and I ran onto it and kicked it and it screamed into the opposing goal. As soon as this happened everything disappeared and I was back on the field playing in the same soccer game. As soon as I was back the exact soccer play that I had just seen occurred. It was identical to what I had just viewed on that huge screen with not a hair's difference and I scored the identical goal which turned out to be the winning match goal. So this play happened about thirty seconds after I had seen it on the big screen.

I am still amazed every time I think about what happened that evening. I put this experience in the same category as premonitions because that is when a medium tells of an event that will occur in the future and then it does actually happen. So the obvious questions is, does the future already exist?

7

CHAPTER

SPIRIT HEALS MY SON

It was early fall of 1996 when I was first introduced to spiritual healing in a most amazing way. I got home from work late at about nine at night. My wife Barbara met me at the front door and she was clearly upset. She proceeded to tell me that our youngest son, Richard, who was 11 years old at the time was in bed crying because of a severe headache. She had given him all the medication she could and nothing had worked. I remember being tired and hungry and thinking that we could be up all night with this poor kid. My wife and I went to his bedroom and he was a pitiful sight, sitting in bed and his face full of tears. I said, "Hi Richard!" He just said, "Dad, this is really bad." Then Spirit took over and I walked over close to him and I put both of my hands on his forehead and in less than a minute he was fast asleep. I did not think anything about what had just happened and we cleaned up his face and covered him up and he slept right through the night. I actually forgot all about it until I got home from work the next evening. Richard was waiting for me and he immediately asked me what I had done to him the night before. I answered that I did not understand. He then said that when I put my hands on his forehead, they were so hot, he was going to ask me to take them away but he said that he does not remember anything after that. I told him he fell asleep and that we just made him comfortable and left him alone to rest. So this was a case where Spirit basically took over my actions and guided me to place my hands on my son's forehead and Spirit sent the healing through me to him.

I did not know about spiritual healing before this incident but now I was on a quest to learn all I could about it. For the record, at the time of this writing my son Richard is 36 years old and he has never had a migraine headache since that healing from Spirit 24 years ago. This wonderful event prompted me to research spiritual healing and during that time I heard of a world-renowned healer by the name of Harry Edwards. I was intrigued by his life story and I learned so much about spiritual healing from reading about his healing work. His healing work continues to this day by his chosen successors at the Harry Edwards Spiritual Healing Sanctuary at Burrows Lea Shere in the United Kingdom. I will devote a chapter to spiritual healing later in this book and the truly amazing healings that spirit allowed me to be a part of.

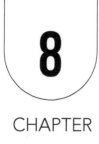

8

CHAPTER

MY MOTHER'S PASSING

Early July 2004 I got a call from my family in Ireland to say that Mum was in hospital because she had suffered four small heart attacks and that I should be ready to fly home on short notice. It was arranged with the hospital that my mum had access to a phone and I talked to her just about every day. Mum was stable but was very fragile and one day my oldest sister called me and asked me what I knew. She was aware that I had some psychic abilities and she was asking me what was going to happen to mum. I was quite annoyed at the question and I told her that I knew nothing more than anyone else and furthermore I would not want to. A couple of nights later when I went to bed my dad appeared to me and he had my mother with him. I was astonished at what I was seeing and also very sad as I thought my mum had passed away and she was now in the spirit world with Dad. My dad then said this to me: "Richard, you know that your mum is very sick and it is time for her to come to our place." I said I understood. He then said that Mum was going to get better for a little while but it is time for her to come to his place. Then he and Mum were gone. I called my older sister the next morning, which was Monday, and told her exactly what had happened. Two days later my sister called me to say they had released Mum from the hospital and she was home and in great form. She said that Mum was out in the garden visiting her flowers and enjoying them very much. I reminded my sister about what Dad had said about Mum getting better for a little while, but she did not want to hear that now, as she said Mum had not looked this good for a very long time. Two days later and it is now Friday, my sister called to say mum was back in hospital and very sick. Right away my mum fell into a coma and she never did recover and she passed away six weeks later on September 1, 2004.

My wife and I went home to Ireland and spent two weeks by my mother's bedside. The night we flew in to Dublin we stopped at the hospital before we went to the family home. We stood by Mum's bed and I told her that I was here with Barbara, my wife, and also that her grandchildren in Canada send their love to her. Now, I was not sure if mum could hear me or not because she was in a deep coma and she could not even move her little finger according to the doctor. It was late at night so I said to my mum that we were going to go home and get some rest and we would be back in the morning. I told Mum I was going to give her a kiss goodnight and as I leaned down to her she puckered her lips for me to kiss her. That was a magical moment for me as I knew for sure that she could hear everything I and everyone said to her. As I visited Mum every day for the next two weeks I could tell her all about her grandchildren in Canada who she had met on a few occasions. Knowing that Mum could hear what I was telling her made it a little easier for me when I had to leave and return to my family and home in Canada. The last thing I said to my mum as I left her bedside on the way to the airport was this. I said, "Mum, feel free to go when you are ready and I will see you in heaven one day."

To explain how it was possible for Dad, who was deceased, to be able to come to me and have Mum with him before she was deceased was something I learned later in my spiritual studies. When a person is gravely ill and is basically bedridden like my mum, the Spirit can and does leave the body and can go back and forth between the spirit world and Earth. That is how my mum accompanied my dad and they both visited me together on that night. There is what is called the 'silver cord' that keeps the spirit of each person tethered to each other and death only comes when the silver cord is severed and the spirit and the body split forever. This is the reason that people have reported seeing a relative before they have actually passed, and wondered how that could happen.

9

CHAPTER

JOINING A SPIRITUALIST CHURCH

It was early 2005 and I had an appointment with a lady at her condominium to measure for new floorcovering. She met me in the lobby of the building and the first thing she said to me was she knew I was the person who she was to meet as soon as I entered the building. I did not really take much notice of her comment as we did have an appointment and I was on time. We took the elevator up to the floor of her new place and when she unlocked the door and let me in she closed the door and leaned against it with her back and she began to give me the most amazingly accurate reading about myself. She started by saying that I was very psychic and that I was a great healer. She also said that I have received information and teaching at night when I slept. I was astonished at the accuracy of everything she told me. I chatted with her at length and I asked her what I can do with these abilities as I had no one to teach me. She told me to join a spiritualist church and to sit in a development circle. Up to that point I did not even know that such a place existed. I looked into this and discovered that there was a spiritualist church of Edmonton.

The wonderful lady that had given me that incredible reading was a medium and she immigrated to Canada from England.

I was truly blessed to meet her as she was the one who set me on the right track to developing these phenomenal faculties that Spirit has blessed me with. I do not have her name but I would love to give her a huge thank you for the very important part she played in my life. I have also learned that spirit brings the people to you that are needed in your life. Like when the student is ready the teacher appears. Just after this I attended my first service at a spiritualist church. It was very different in a refreshing way from the traditional religious services and I also received a message from my deceased brother-in-law from one of the mediums. I came back the next week to service and on the third week the minister said to me that they thought I would have shown up to Thursday evening circle. I replied that I was not aware of the circle and also that I would not just show up unless I was invited. The minister said that it was an open door circle and everyone who is interested is welcome to join in. I joined the open circle the very next week and began the next phase of my spiritual journey. It was difficult at first because I had never actually been taught how to meditate properly. I was given the basic instructions and I began to learn meditation. I was told that the reason we learn to meditate is to quieten our mind and in the quietness we will learn to hear Spirit. I had always heard Spirit and when Spirit needed me to see them they were able to make that happen but for the most part I could hear Spirit but I could not see them. The purpose for sitting in a circle is to develop your mediumship to the highest level that you can so that you can connect to those living in the spirit world and receive information that is accurate and can be validated by the person the spirit has come through for. This is why it is called a development circle and the more you attend and sit in a circle the more you learn. And the better your mediumship becomes. Unless you are a completely natural born medium, and there are a few in the world, you have to work hard at your development. You have to be dedicated to sit in a circle at least once a week for many years because everyone develops at their own pace. Your spirit guide is always with you and there to help you but I can promise you one thing for sure and that is, Spirit will not allow you to learn something and move forward in your development until they know you are ready to do so.

This brings to mind another important point and that is, it is impossible for anyone to take a weekend course as a beginner and then declare themselves to be a medium. It just does not work that way and this is very unethical. I have been sitting in circles for over sixteen years and teaching for about eleven years and I will continue to belong to a development circle for the rest of my life on Earth. The reason for this is that I want to continue to learn as much as I can and I want to continually improve my mediumship. We know from spiritual teachings that there is no end to learning and so as I continue to learn my overall mediumship becomes stronger and this allows me to be of greater service to Spirit. It is my belief that this beautiful, sacred, and divine faculty was given to us so that we can be in service to spirit and this can only be achieved through ethical mediumship.

10

CHAPTER

MEETING SILVER BIRCH

It was about four months after I joined my first development circle at the Spiritualist Church of Edmonton and I was doing well at learning to meditate. At least I was able to somewhat quieten my mind and sit in meditation for a short time. In the beginning, meditation for ten minutes felt like it was an hour in length but with practice it gets easier and so much more enjoyable. On this evening our circle leader told us to relax and go into meditation and when we were called back, usually in about ten minutes, each member would then share their experience and as a group we would have a discussion on what had taken place for each circle member. One of the most amazing and life changing events was about to take place for me.

As I closed my eyes to begin meditation, I immediately found myself high above the Earth with a beautiful golden eagle flying beside me. As I looked down, all I could see was green trees and I casually remember thinking that we were flying across the beautiful forests of Canada. Next I saw a tiny white object way ahead in the distance and instinctively I knew we were headed there. Almost immediately we were coming down to land and I remember looking down at the ground to make sure my feet were positioned properly for a safe landing. After I landed safely, I looked up and my eagle had landed and was perched on the branch of a nearby tree. The white object I had seen was in fact a tepee and there was an Indigenous man standing in front of it. He said to me, "Hello, my name is Silver Birch." I was just about to answer him when our circle leader interrupted by calling us all back to the room. I was totally annoyed as I wanted to have a conversation with this person called Silver Birch who I had never heard of before this. When it came to my turn to share my experience, everyone became silent as I related my story to them. I noticed how quiet everyone was and so I asked if they had ever heard of this person. Our circle leader, who was also the minister of the church, said yes, they knew who he was. I immediately asked if they would tell me about him. Her reply was that there was too much to tell and they thought I should read about him. Now, the minister's mother was a circle member and she had taken a liking to me and she said that she had the complete collection of the Silver Birch books. She said that she would lend them to me on one condition, that as I finished reading each book I was to return it to her and only her. These books were precious to her as when she purchased them she had to send to England for them as that was the only place they were available from at that time. I gratefully accepted her offer and promised to return each book to her into her hands only. The following week on circle night she brought a small soft bag containing the Silver Birch books. She gave them to me at the close of our circle that evening and I was so excited I could hardly wait to get home and take a look at the books. When I arrived home I immediately went to my bedroom and I opened the bag and poured all the books out onto my bed. The Silver Birch books all have a different title and so I was not sure which book I should read first or in what order they were written in. I decided to just close my eyes and pick one and leave it to fate. I did just that and when I opened the cover of the book, I discovered the lady who owned the books had put a sticker on them which said 'this book belongs to the library of: (her name).' The stickers came with a small picture attached to it and this particular picture was of a golden eagle perched on a branch of a tree with a white tepee and an Indigenous man standing in front of it. I was truly astonished as this picture was identical in every way to the scene I had witnessed when I first met Silver Birch the previous week during our circle meditation.

When I finished reading all of the Silver Birch books and returned them to their owner I felt I had received a great education of spiritual knowledge as these books are written in simple form and are very easy to understand. For me the most pleasing and satisfying thing about the content of these books is knowing that it all came from the spirit world through Silver Birch as he spoke through his medium. The medium who served Silver Birch for about sixty years was Maurice Barbanell and they had a most remarkable partnership until the passing of the medium in July of 1981. Maurice Barbanell was a trance medium and so to prepare for his guide to work with him he would lie down on a couch and fall into a trance. His guide, Silver Birch, would then take control and speak using the medium's voice box. There was a very clear difference between the voice of the medium and that of the spirit guide. In those days these meetings were called séances and everything that Silver Birch said was recorded by designated people who wrote it all down. The Silver Birch books I am talking about contain all or most of everything that was written down during these séances many years ago. This is why they are such a treasure of spiritual knowledge and they are not just the musings of someone on Earth.

A couple of my favourite pieces of advice to the world from Silver Birth are as follows: He says spirituality is the coin of service. He also reminds us that everything comes from Spirit, through Spirit, to spirit. I consider myself very honoured, blessed, and privileged for the amazing meeting I had with Silver Birch. He is and always will be the most influential spiritual teacher in my life. His teachings are so very simple, yet so very profound. If you have an open mind or are curious about spiritualism or life after death I would recommend that you read any of the Silver Birch books.

They are truly amazing and uplifting and you will find answers to your most puzzling questions on these subjects. My meeting with Silver Birch was planned and organised by those in the spirit world that are capable of performing such duties. Not only have I learned about this from the teachings of Silver Birch but ever since that first meeting he has been a regular influence in my life. To make something very clear, I am not saying he is my spirit guide because he is not. I know and have a great relationship with my own spirit guide, but Silver Birch has taken an interest in my life in order to help me wherever he sees that is needed. As my story continues it will become very obvious as to what I mean by that.

11

CHAPTER

MY LEARNING CONTINUES

As the weeks passed I became more comfortable sitting in circle. My confidence grew as I began to see grey images at first and then they became clearer and I could make out the features of the spirits that were coming through. Eventually my vision of the spirit people and what they would show and tell me became more like a video with full colour. This was very exciting for me as I was now able to connect with spirit and receive evidential information from them for my fellow circle members. I did learn one very hard but valuable lesson at the beginning of my mediumship. When I gave my first good message in our circle I was so excited that I told spirit to bring it on. In response to me spirit stopped me in my tracks, and for the next three months I sat in circle and I could not get anything from spirit. My teachers in the spirit world were showing me that they are always in charge and they will decide when I am ready to move forward. I learned that Spirit will never give you anything until you are ready for it. It was tough sitting in our circle for that long and trying to connect but getting nowhere. Our circle had now become closed, which meant that there would be no new people allowed to join and the other factor was that if anyone had poor attendance they would be asked to leave permanently, so my only choices were to leave the group or stay and learn my lesson. I stayed, of course, and eventually Spirit began to work with me again. An important lesson learned that I have never forgotten.

My progress continued and after about a year my teacher would ask me to join her on the platform to give one message when she would hold an 'Evening with Spirit' event, which is an all message service with those who live in the spirit world. This helped to prepare me for what was to come down the road. One evening an Indigenous lady came to the church to ask for help in locating her husband, who had gone missing. Our circle teacher asked all of us to have a go at trying to locate him by connecting to those in the spirit world who were related to this gentleman. None of us were successful but when everyone had left the church that evening I noticed that outside the front door of the church was a small cloud or fog just sitting under the outdoor light. It was most peculiar as everywhere else there was no fog; in fact, it was a beautiful clear fall evening. I was drawn to this apparition and I went outside and walked under the light, and as I did this I was given a message which said that the missing man was safe and with someone named Francis. I then went back inside and told my teacher what had just taken place. She and I and the rest of our circle went back to check out this mysterious fog but it had vanished and there was no sign of any fog nearby. My teacher relayed the information to the missing man's family the next morning and sure enough he was located at the home of a relative named Francis in northern Alberta. I found this to be an extraordinary but wonderful teaching that Spirit had provided me with. I also remember that I was not afraid to go and stand in this fog. It was like Spirit guided me to do this and I knew I would be safe. I have learned over the years that when Spirit comes to you they bring with them a beautiful calming energy which relaxes you and dispels all fear.

I continued to sit in circle and attended all services for three years until the church closed its doors. I had another beautiful experience with Spirit during that time and it was about the birth of our first grandchild. My eldest son Mark and his wife Nancy were having trouble conceiving and they had been trying for a few years including help from their doctor. Mark and Nancy had gone to Ireland for their honeymoon and one of my aunties gave them a statue of a very famous character from Dublin called Molly Malone. In their home back in Edmonton they placed the statue on the mantelpiece of their fireplace in their living room. It is important to note that the fireplace was built into the corner of the room and a couple of feet away there was a large window which went almost to the floor level and this was completely covered with curtains. It was a Friday evening and Mark and Nancy arrived home from work and they were shocked and a little scared to find the statue from the fireplace was sitting on the windowsill inside the curtains. If the statue which was made of ceramic had somehow fallen off the mantelpiece it would have surely been broken and or damaged the windowsill because there was a distance of about four feet down from the top of the fireplace to the windowsill. The statue looked like it was gently placed inside the curtains and the image of Molly Malone was facing looking out the window. Mark called me in a bit of a panic and told me what they had found and asked what could be going on. I told him to calm down and I would connect with Spirit and see if I could get any answers. I hung up the phone and started to walk down my hallway to my bedroom where it would be quiet for me to work with Spirit. I was still in my hallway when this voice from Spirit interrupted me and said, "Of course it was me who moved the statue, because I knew they would call you. Please tell them that there is a beautiful baby coming to them." I then realised that this was my Aunt Eileen speaking to me from the spirit world. Aunt Eileen was my favourite aunt of all and she was the one that gave Mark and Nancy the statue for a wedding present and now she had come to give them this wonderful news. She had passed away a couple of years after their wedding. I went back into my kitchen and shared the news with my wife Barbara but she asked me not to tell Mark and Nancy about the baby in case I was wrong and it would just be more disappointment and heartbreak for them. I reluctantly agreed, as what she said made sense. I called Mark and told him that it was Aunt Eileen just saying hello and to let you know that she is around you. Mark immediately asked me if she had said anything else and I told him no.

Lying to my son, especially about a message from Spirit just did not sit well with me and it bothered me all weekend. Finally on the Sunday I explained to my wife that this was not proper and that I had no right to keep this message from them. I called the kids and gave them the message and they understood why I did not share it at first. It turned out that Nancy had an appointment with her gynaecologist in two days' time, on Tuesday, and there she would discover that she was pregnant. The following February 10, 2007 their beautiful daughter Ceiligh was born.

12

CHAPTER

MY FIRST MEDIUMSHIP READINGS

After I had been sitting in the development circle I wanted to try to do a private reading, so I asked my daughter-in-law Nancy if she would allow me to practice doing a reading for her. She agreed and we made a date for a Sunday afternoon. Nancy arrived at my home and she had brought a photograph of someone sealed inside an envelope. She did this because at that time I had practiced this type of connection in my circle where we were given an envelope containing a photo of someone who had passed on and we would try and connect with them and get accurate information from them. I held the envelope in my hand and it did not take long until I could see a gentleman and he said he was Nancy's grandfather. He gave me lots of information that Nancy could identify and some information that she had to check with her mother, as this grandfather was her mother's dad. A week later, on the following Sunday, Nancy went to visit her mom and she asked her about the information that I had received from the grandfather that she did not know about. Nancy's mom was shocked and asked Nancy how she knew this information. Nancy then told her mom that I, her father-in-law was learning to be a medium and about the reading I had done for her. Nancy's mom was now even more surprised by this because only two days before she had found a diary that her dad had kept and the information that Nancy was inquiring about was there in this diary, written down in her dad's handwriting. This was incredible evidence for me as Nancy's grandfather had come through with this information five days before his diary was found and so his granddaughter knew about this information before his daughter did even though Nancy could not confirm it until she asked her mother about it. As for me, this was amazing proof of life after death and the ability of mediums to be able to contact and communicate with our loved ones in the spirit world.

Nancy's brother Neil and his wife Jenn were also having trouble starting a family. They did not have any trouble conceiving but Jenn miscarried every time for a total of five times. This was very hard on them emotionally and so they applied for adoption even though Jenn was pregnant for the fifth time. Nancy asked Jenn if she would be interested in a spiritual healing and Jenn said that she would try anything. Jenn came to me and I gave her a healing from Spirit but she still miscarried again. That healing took place sometime in the summer of 2006. Around the middle of March 2007 Neil and Jenn decided they would like a reading and so they came to my home and Nancy accompanied them to take notes of their reading so they could look over them later. The spirits that came through as I remember were recognised mostly by Neil but just as I was winding up the reading, Spirit told me to tell them that a baby was coming to them at the end of March. That was my final statement to them which ended the reading. Later I asked Nancy if they had enjoyed the readings and she said that it was very good and interesting but they said I was totally wrong about the arrival of a baby. Jenn said that she was not pregnant and that they had only very recently applied for adoption and were told it would take quite a bit of time as they would have to go on a waiting list and there were many couples ahead of them. Well, Spirit is never wrong when they make a specific statement like they did and on March 31, 2007 Neil and Jenn received their first child—a beautiful baby boy. There were some unusual circumstances about this particular adoption which are private to Neil and Jenn that made this baby available to them so quickly. Neil and Jenn wanted a second child and were on a waiting list for a long time. They were considering changing adoption agencies, which would mean forfeiting the adoption fees that were quite substantial. Nancy called me on their behalf to see if I could offer any advice. I sat with Spirit and asked what they should do and I was told that they should stay with the same agency. Nancy relayed the message to Neil and Jenn and they took the advice. They were very happy they did as it was not too long after that they received a call from the agency and they adopted a gorgeous baby girl. This made them very happy and thankful as it completed their lovely family. So, as you can see, my first couple of readings were very evidential and extraordinary and of course boosted my confidence that I could actually connect to Spirit in a strong manner.

13

CHAPTER

LIFE-ALTERING EXPERIENCE

I continued being a church member and sitting in circle and even got involved in helping to run the church service. I was very happy with all that I was learning until one evening late in the fall of 2007, when I arrived at the church for our weekly circle meeting only to be told that the church was closing its doors for good. I was completely taken by surprise, shocked and devastated. The minister asked me what I was going to do and I answered that I did not know but I added that this was not something I could just give up doing as it was a major part of my life now. There was no reason given to us as to why the church was closing after being in existence for over ninety-five years and as I was not a board member I did not have any authority to question the motive. After I gathered my thoughts I told the minister and my circle members that I would use my home to keep the circle going. The minister said she would relay that information to those that were not present and then I left and went with a very heavy heart. It took a couple of weeks to organise, but soon we had our circle up and running and in no time the word spread and we were almost over capacity. The circle went very well given my inexperience and after a year one of the ladies attending volunteered the use of her home to run the circle at. This turned out to be a great idea as some circle members had a bit of a journey each week to attend circle at my home and this move would now reverse that and I and some other members would now have to travel to attend circle at this new location. It turned out to be a very fair arrangement and everyone was happy. The host of the circle also knew a very wonderful spiritual teacher who had a great deal of experience running circles and had convinced her to help us out by becoming our circle leader. I shall call her Sharon Ames and she would become a very important person in my life

Sharon ran our circle for about six months and then, as sometimes happens, the circle came to an end for one reason or another. But before it ended I had another amazing experience with Spirit. One day after circle, Sharon asked me if I would give her a healing and I said of course I would. She told me that when she sits for a couple of hours at a time one of her ankles and foot seizes up and it takes her some time to loosen it up so she can walk again. As we were all about to leave our circle host's home, I told Sharon that I would do the healing when I got to my own house. It was later that evening when I sat down with my healing guides to ask them to send healing to Sharon and as soon as I made the request Spirit said to me she needs an adjustment. I continued with the healing and thought nothing more of it. The next morning Sharon called me and said, "Richard, you did the healing, didn't you?" I replied that I had and she said that she was sitting at her computer desk and without warning her foot was physically turned by an invisible force. She knew this was Spirit and she added that her foot was feeling much better already. Sharon then went on to tell me that she had been going to her chiropractor for over a year and he was not able to fix the problem. Sharon went back to her chiropractor to ask him if he would advise her on what kind of exercises she should do to strengthen her leg muscles because she had been favouring using her other leg more because of the problem with her foot and ankle. Sharon had stopped going to her chiropractor for quite some time because he was not making any progress, and because of this he insisted on taking an X-ray of her foot. When he saw the X-ray he came back to the room where

Sharon was waiting for the results. He was not very happy and asked her what other doctor she had been seeing. She assured him that she had not gone to any other doctor and then he produced her original X-ray which was over a year old and the new X-ray and he said these are different, you have had an adjustment. When I heard those words I remembered Spirit telling me the exact same thing as I was doing the healing for Sharon. This was a beautiful and amazing spiritual experience that Sharon and I were privileged to share together.

Then when our circle broke up, Sharon and I got together and we would work with Spirit just the two of us. We were discussing what the future held for each of us and I told her that I was thinking of opening up a spiritual centre because I felt it was needed here in Edmonton. Sharon then told me she had run a spiritual centre for many years in the past and as we spoke about this we decided that if we could find a cheap rental space that we could share, it might be a good place for me to start. Both of us thought that this was a good idea and so we set about looking for a premises. We eventually found a suitable small location on the south side of Edmonton for a very reasonable cost. It would prove to work out great as Sharon did all of her work there during the daytime and I ran my development circles in the evening and my church service on Sunday morning. So when each of us were there we had the complete area to ourselves.

14

CHAPTER

OPENING ST. BRIGID'S SPIRITUAL CENTRE

When we found our leasing space we were given a month to clean it up and give it a clean coat of paint. I began thinking of a name for the centre and I was looking up Celtic names but I could not settle on any one completely. A few weeks prior to this, as we sat together with Spirit, my grandmother Lanigan who I always called Nana kept coming to me and she had a coy smile on her face which said, *I know something you don't know.* When this happened a few times in a row I had this strong feeling that I wanted to remember my Nana's name. I could not recall it as I hardly ever heard it or used it while I was growing up. When I visited her it was usually with my dad and he of course would call her mum. Then one day I went to a lady's home in Edmonton to do some work and when she answered the door she greeted me with a lovely smile and said, "You must be Richard, my name is Brigette." I immediately remembered that my Nana's name was Brigid, which sounds the same as the lady's except with the Irish way of spelling it. I was very happy that I now remembered my Nana's name but I was not sure why I needed to know. Meanwhile, Sharon was on my case because we were close to opening the centre and I did not have a name for it yet. Then a day or so after I discovered my Nana's name, Sharon asked me if

I ever had considered using the name of Saint Brigid. I was very surprised that this lovely Canadian lady from Montreal even knew anything about Saint Brigid of Ireland, who is the second patron saint of our country. Sharon had learned about Brigid during her studies of world religions. I then told Sharon about my Nana Brigid who had visited me in our circle and the lady who I went to work for was named Brigette. Sharon smiled and said, "Richard, this is Spirit's way of giving you the name for your centre." And so, St. Brigid's Spiritual Centre was created. So I had the name and then I applied for and received our business licence and we opened on July 4, 2009.

It was tough going in the beginning as we were brand new and without the means to pay for advertising. Many times my wife and I would be at the centre on a Sunday morning for our service and we would have three or four people show up and on other occasions nobody would show. Things gradually got better and I had a development circle on Wednesday evenings which was quite successful. We were at this location for two years but Sharon had left after about a year to pursue other interests. This was my starting place, but I always had in the back of my mind that our location should be in the west end of Edmonton. Again, I am sure that Spirit had placed that thought in my mind and on the very last day of my lease at our south side location, my leasing agent called me and told me about a great deal on a space in the west end of Edmonton. I went to see the place and it was perfect. It had more room and was in a great location, but it was going to cost me twelve hundred dollars a month. I trusted that Spirit brought me to this location and so I signed a two-year lease not knowing how I was going to afford it. I was earning decent money at my trade and so the worst thing that could happen would be that I would have to subsidise it out of my own pocket because overnight my monthly lease went from six hundred dollars to twelve hundred.

During my years I had got to know some good local psychics and mediums and one of them had asked me to do some platform work on a couple of occasions, so I called her and asked her if she was willing to do this with me once a month to help with raising funds to pay our rent. She agreed and all of a sudden I was thrust into working publicly as a medium. I was used to giving a mediumship demonstration at the end of every Sunday service but I must admit this was a bit daunting as our event would be called an Evening with Spirit and we would be working for two straight hours. Despite my opening-night jitters, everything went well and so this became a monthly event and most times it would pay for over half of our rent. The balance of our rent came from our collection at our Sunday service and our circle members. Everything it takes to run a spiritual centre or church is voluntary, no one gets paid and so we rely on our community for donations at Sunday service and our circle members who pay a weekly fee to sit and learn and develop together. We have our ups and downs but these are just learning curves that happen in almost every part of society where groups of people gather for a common cause. People will always have different opinions on any given subject and sometimes this leads to unhappiness and in-house disagreements. Then there are the people who join groups of any denomination with their own agenda in mind. My wonderful friend Sharon warned me about this when she told me to be careful with who I trust because she said there are those who wait until someone builds something and then they will try to take it away from you. Sharon would know, as she had run her own spiritual centre for about fourteen years and had experienced this first hand. Well, sadly she was perfectly right and this has happened three times since we opened in eleven years. Fortunately the good guys prevailed and as we have grown and learned we have become a stronger and smarter group and have implemented rules and regulations to prevent this happening in the future.

15

CHAPTER

MOVING FORWARD

In the fall of 2007 I had the opportunity to attend a live performance of an international medium. He gave an excellent demonstration of mediumship and I actually received a great message from my mother and father who were now in spirit. He also did one thing that I was very impressed with and I had not ever seen any other medium do before. He had gone to a gift shop in the hotel he was staying in and purchased a small gift to give to an audience member at his event that evening. He had asked Spirit to direct him as to what gift he should buy. During his demonstration he was drawn to a lady and he delivered information and a message from a loved one in Spirit and also the gift he had purchased. He asked that lady if she knew the significance of the gift he was led to buy for her and she was in tears as she said she fully understood why her loved one in Spirit would want her to have this present. As I said, I was very impressed and a short time later I asked spirit if I could incorporate this into my mediumship for our monthly Evening with Spirit events at St. Brigid's. Those in the spirit world heard my request and they granted my wish with a little twist. The first time I sat with Spirit to ask them to guide me to buy a gift for someone who would be attending our Evening with Spirit they showed me a bouquet of flowers. I said, *Okay* and I went to a local flower shop and I was surprised to find a bouquet of flowers that looked very like the ones that Spirit had shown me earlier that day. I purchased the flowers and during our mediumship demonstration that evening I was able to connect to a spirit who wished to give these flowers to their loved one in our audience. This was a beautiful event that Spirit allowed me to be a part of and the lady who received them was simply amazed and overjoyed. I made this a part of our monthly Evening with Spirit event and Spirit has never let me down. Over the years there have been times when I would have to purchase two or three bouquets of flowers all different from each other and we have always been able to find who in the audience they are for by connecting with their loved ones in Spirit. Many times we have two or three mediums working the same event and I would simply describe the kind and colours of the flowers that Spirit had shown me earlier that day. The other mediums had to be aware of this because the Spirit belonging to the person who is to receive the flowers may choose to come through them and give them the information about which flowers they were to present to their loved one. All of our mediums participated in presenting flowers and I believe they really enjoyed that. It is precious to see the joy on the faces of those who receive flowers from their family and friends who now reside in the spirit world. For me this is more irrefutable proof that our loved ones in the spirit world are always around us and have an interest in what we are doing.

When I sit with Spirit on the day of our demonstrations it is usually six or seven hours before the event begins and Spirit shows me how many bouquets of flowers to buy including what type of flowers and the colours of them. You see, your loved ones in Spirit know you are going to attend our event because they hear you talking about it and planning it. The evidence is very assuring to the people who are present that their loved ones in the spirit world are always close by and around us. On some occasions Spirit shows me a type of flower that actually should not be in season at that particular time of year but when I go to the flower shop it is usually the first flower I see. I was told to buy yellow tulips in January one time and they were front and centre in the flower shop when I went there to purchase them. I presented them to a lady that evening who had come to our demonstration that night for the very first time. Her neighbour who had passed away only a month earlier came through to her with these flowers. They were good friends and she always admired his front lawn where he grew yellow tulips every year. She was amazed at this beautiful way her neighbour and friend came through for her.

On another occasion Spirit showed me a bouquet of tulips which were beautiful but very unique. They were pure white with the slightest colour of pink all around the tip of the flower. I had never seen tulips like this before and really thought I had my work cut out for me to find them, but I was wrong because they were the first flowers I noticed as I entered the flower shop. That evening I presented them to a young woman whose husband had passed away. She was brought to our Evening with Spirit by a friend of hers in the hope that her husband would come through. This lady was not quite sure about how this all worked but she understood the information her husband gave me for her. When the evening came to an end she came to me and asked me to explain about the flowers. I told her how I get the information earlier in the day from Spirit and then I go and purchase the flowers and bring them to the demonstration that evening. She also asked why these flowers were so special. I told her that I did not understand her question as I just buy the flowers that Spirit shows me. I then said to her that the flowers usually mean something to the person who receives them and she then said that these were the same flowers that were put on her husband's grave. I explained to her that this was her husband's way of telling her that it was truly him that gave her these flowers. The tears flowed freely now but they were tears of joy as she realised that her husband was around her and sending his love to her.

16

CHAPTER

MY SACRED PLACE

One of the most wonderful and beautiful things that my friend Sharon taught me was to ask my spirit guide to create a special place for us to meet. She explained that I should meditate for a short time just to relax myself and then ask my spirit guide to create this special place for us. This was at a time when it was just Sharon and myself that were sitting together with Spirit and just before I opened Saint Brigid's Spiritual Centre. So the same evening that Sharon suggested this to me I decided to do it as my lesson for that night. We did a short meditation and then I asked my spirit guide to create a special meeting place for us. I sat with my guide for about half an hour and the only thing that happened was that I found myself sitting alone in some space but I could not see anything. I continued to do this on a weekly basis and for three months nothing changed or happened except the longer I went to this place I began to feel that I was in some type of room and I felt like I was always sitting at a very large round table. I also felt that this table had a huge hole in the middle of it, so large that I thought there was hardly any edge to the table. I remember thinking to myself that this was a very stupid table because there was not enough room of the edge to place a cup of tea on it. Now, remember I still could not see anything but I was just sensing or feeling these things. Just at the end of three months sitting in this place I went there as usual and I got an amazing surprise. I went to my place and I was finally shown what it looked like. I was sitting in a very large tepee and the round table I thought I was sitting at was the place where the Indigenous people would have their sweats. I of course was sitting by the edge of where the heated stones were and all of a sudden I began floating up with the steam from the heated rocks and I went right out of the top of the tepee. As I continued floating up outside, every time I and the steam touched a tree or rock face of the small mountain that was there the face of an Indigenous elder appeared to me. It was mysterious, mesmerising and a totally amazing spiritual experience that I shall never forget. I now knew that my sacred place was a beautiful big tepee created by my spirit guide for us to meet in and learn spiritual truths.

When I discovered this I was not totally surprised because, although I was born in Ireland, I always felt a real attraction to the Indigenous people of Canada. Every time after that when I would go to my sacred place I would see my tepee and when I walked up to it the flap on the outside entrance would be lifted up for me to enter but I never could see who would do this. I always looked forward to going there and meeting my guide and seeing what would be there to discover. Many times we would meet other spirit beings and other times we would just sit in each other's company. One nice surprise happened as I approached the entrance to our tepee, my dad stepped forward and lifted the flap to allow me to enter. I thought this was nice of my dad to visit me but he made a habit of this and soon he became a permanent fixture there to let me enter. Not long after this I went to a workshop for mediumship development and on the last day I was partnered with one of the teachers to work with. She gave me a wonderful reading and brought my dad through, who said that he was now on my healing team. That explained to me why he was very visible to me now, and when I get ready to work with Spirit, especially for healing, I always catch a glimpse of him. It's like he is making sure that I knew he is part of the healing team and is backing me up. On another occasion at my sacred place when I was sitting there with my guide, four Indigenous men came running in at a slow pace and they stopped just over to the right of where I was sitting. I welcomed them and invited them to sit down. One of them replied to me by saying, "We are your healing guides and we just want you to meet us." I thanked them and then they left and I would not get to see them for another eleven years. It was a wonderful gift from Spirit as I now knew who my main healing guides were; even if I could not see them anymore, I could envision them every time I called on them to perform spiritual healing.

I had another amazing and beautiful being visit me in my sacred place shortly after I met my healing guides. I was sitting in the company of my spirit guide when this brilliantly bright being appeared directly in front of me. It was a being made of light and it looked like it was made of clear diamonds and it was dazzling as it moved towards me. I remember thinking, *If it comes too close to me, I won't be able to continue looking at it because of its brightness.* To my surprise it came right up to me and I could still look at it without being blinded. This beautiful spiritual being did not say anything to me and then it just disappeared. Later on as I sat thinking about my mysterious beautiful visitor, I did not know how to refer to it, so I called it The Shining One. That is how I would describe my experience to my fellow colleagues and students. About a year later I was reading a spiritual book of which I cannot recall the name now and this book had a description of light beings that they called The Shining Ones. The description of the light beings was the same as the one that visited me in my sacred place. I did not know at the time that I met this light being that it would be eleven more years until I would meet them again.

Another experience I had in my sacred place happened as I entered my tepee and there was an open tunnel just to the left of the entrance. I asked my guide what it was doing there and he said it was for my use. He told me that anytime I wanted to go to the spirit world and visit that I should use this tunnel. I decided to try this and on my first journey there I learned how to use the tunnel. I remember stepping into the tunnel and instead of walking I was suddenly floating in it. At the beginning it was a little dark and as I floated in further it started getting brighter and then I came out the other end into a glorious bright place and I was in a lovely open green meadow. Then Spirit told me that I could experience anything I wanted. I asked Spirit for my ideal home if I could have my wish. My perfect place would be a modest house on the beach of a beautiful ocean with a forest close by as well. I was immediately at this place and I just remember being so happy and blissful. Upon coming back to Earth I wrote down my experience. I used the tunnel for quite a few trips and always wrote of my experience immediately on my return to Earth. I called them 'lessons from the light'. One of my failings in life is that when I discover something new I pay full attention to it and after a while when the novelty of it wears off I go on to something new. The great thing about it though, is I know the tunnel is always available to me and I will use it again at another time.

As I get older, I appreciate the amazing experiences and teachings I have received from Spirit and I feel very honoured and privileged to be able to be in service to Spirit. I also now have a clear idea of what I am to focus on for the rest of my life. As I write this it is November of 2020 and Spirit has spoken directly to me and told me the reason I came to Earth this time. This has also been validated by a couple of amazing mediums I know when I had them do readings for me. I visit my sacred place almost every day because that is where I do all of my spiritual work from. I join my spirit team there and I request the help from them that I need for the particular service that I need to provide. For example, if I have a request for a healing then I ask that my main healing guides join me with the healing team. There are many spirit healers on the team but the healing is organised by the four main guides who I spoke about earlier. If I am to do a mediumship reading I ask my main spirit guide to work with me as well as the spirit people who would be friends or family of the person who requested the reading. So just to make it clear about one's spirit team, it would consist of the following: If you are a healer you will have healing guides and many other spirit healers who make up your healing team, and from what I understand the more healing you become involved in the more healers become attracted to you and so your healing team grows. You also have your main spirit guide, who is with you from the moment you are born until you cross over into spirit again, along with helpers and teachers who will constantly change as your mediumship grows. You may also be assigned highly evolved spirit teachers to guide you if you came to Earth to complete a special mission.

17

CHAPTER

A MOST BEAUTIFUL GIFT FROM SPIRIT

It was late October or early November 2012 when I received an inquiry from a lady in Australia about St. Brigid's Spiritual Centre. She informed me that she and her family were relocating to Edmonton in early January 2013 and was wondering if we would be open in the winter. I remember having a quiet chuckle to myself and I promptly replied to her by email assuring her that the country did not close down when winter arrives but that we simply dressed to face the elements. This lovely lady's name is Patricia Strong and she later told me that she smiled at my response but thought I was a cheeky devil. True to her word, Patricia and her family arrived in Edmonton in the first week of January and she and her husband Robert showed up on that Sunday at St. Brigid's to attend our Sunday morning service. When the service finished, Patricia stayed behind to introduce herself to me and have a chat. During our conversation Patricia said that she noticed I was wearing many hats, in other words that I did everything myself. I explained that I was the only minister at the centre and that there was not anyone else qualified enough to run the service. Patricia immediately offered to do the mediumship demonstration for me and I gratefully accepted. Then I told Patricia that we held a development circle every Wednesday evening and invited her to join if she was interested. Patricia accepted my invitation and so our relationship began.

Patricia was not sure exactly how long she would be living in Canada because her husband was here on a work visa and was employed in the oil business and because of that she took advantage of any courses in mediumship that she could attend while she was here. Patricia did take many courses and then brought what she had learned back and shared it with us at St. Brigid's. Everyone at the centre, especially those who were sitting in circles, were the beneficiaries of her knowledge and she soon became the main teacher. I would teach the circles with her and so my knowledge and teaching abilities became stronger because of working with her every week. Patricia did private readings in her own home and it did not take long before she had built up quite a large clientele because of the quality of her readings. She is certainly one of the best spiritual mediums I know and I have had the pleasure of working alongside her for over four years. Things were going along quite nicely but then we had the misfortune of several people at the centre having their own agendas. This resulted in disagreements and eventually the parting of ways with some of our members. The end result was that the only two people left to keep the centre going were Patricia Strong and myself. We had a good heart-to-heart conversation about the situation and Patricia pledged her full support to me to keep the centre going.

We started to work on that and then we decided that if we were going to do this we should change the centre to a church. I always wanted it to be a church but I called it St. Brigid's Spiritual Centre because I did not want any connection made to the previous spiritualist church in our area that closed down under peculiar circumstances. We got the necessary paperwork and changed our name to St. Brigid's Spiritualist Church of Edmonton. Not long after that Patricia informed me that she would like to become a spiritual minister. I was overjoyed with this and as I had the full course that I had studied for my ministry in my possession I gave it to Patricia to study for her ministry and because I was an ordained minister I was qualified to evaluate and mark all of her examination papers. Patricia did her studies and passed all the exams with flying colours. Then both Patricia and I did an additional course through the Spiritualist Church of Canada to fully satisfy their requirements for us both to be accepted as ordained spiritualist ministers. We were happy to do this, as we fully support the great work that they do and we and our church are members of the Spiritualist Church of Canada. Because of our association with them, all of our students can take any course that is offered by them and if successful they can receive a certificate of achievement which are the only legal and recognised certificates in Canada. So under the guidance of the Spiritualist Church of Canada one can, if successful after examination, become a certified spiritualist medium or spiritual healer plus all the certificates that an ordained spiritualist minister receives. We strongly recommend to anyone who is wanting to study spiritualism and the phenomena associated with it that they do it through the Spiritualist Church of Canada or a member spiritualist church. If you do not reside in Canada then look up your local spiritualist church or the governing body of spiritualism in the country you reside in.

So Patricia and I got to work on building a strong spiritual community and as we did our friendship and working relationship went from strength to strength and we truly formed a very special bond. We always had each other's back and we both believe our success was due to the fact that there was not ego between us. Every decision we made was in the best interest of our church and our community. We never argued with each other and at the same time we were always true to ourselves. By that I mean we each had our own opinions on everything and we totally respected each other. I do remember one time as we were doing the Sunday service and a spiritual question was asked and Patricia began by saying that this was something that Richard and I disagree on.

The audience were shocked as they had assumed that we totally agreed on everything. After we both answered the question from our own understanding our community learned a very valuable lesson that morning which was to respect everyone's opinion on any subject because everyone can only answer and react to anything that life presents to us according to their understanding. Patricia and I worked brilliantly together when we did mediumship demonstrations. As she herself put it, we just seemed to roll off each other. We would do the demonstration together every Sunday morning at the end of service and once a month when we hosted an Evening with Spirit at our church. These were two-hour events and we really enjoyed that because we gave evidential mediumship and at the same time we kept it light and funny. Patricia being from Australia and I from Ireland, we not only had different accents but we each brought our own unique humour to it. It was always a great evening enjoyed by all. Together we built a beautiful solid spiritual community and we enjoyed working side by side as a very cohesive team for over four years.

Then one day my worst fears were realised when Patricia told me that she and her family had to return to Australia because of the downturn in Canada's oil industry. I was heartbroken to say the least and could not imagine life without Patricia in it. She was my rock, my guru, and a magnificent friend and between us we had a most special and unique working partnership that I knew could never be replicated. I came to accept this act of fate and it was made easier by knowing I could always contact her if I needed her sage advice. We have always kept in touch with each other and as Patricia has a great love for Canada and for St. Brigid's she has been coming back in the spring and fall each year to visit us and do some work at the church. She continues to have a great following and many clients here in Edmonton who book her up for readings when she visits. When Covid-19 hit the world, we began to do everything virtually and so new and exciting doors opened up for everyone. I have done a few virtual Evenings with

Spirit with Patricia and they were very well received. I found it amazing that it worked so easily as Patricia is in Australia and I in Edmonton and we just co-ordinated the different time zones and the demonstration went off the same as if Patricia and I were on the same platform in the same church. It goes to show that there are no physical barriers to the power of Spirit. It is great technology that allows us to work in this manner but there is nothing like working live with your fellow mediums and audience. I look forward to when Patricia can travel to Canada again and we can do that. And so, as I end this chapter, I will always regard my wonderful friend as a most beautiful gift from Spirit.

18

CHAPTER

ONE DOOR CLOSES, ANOTHER OPENS

Our church was in a good position when we lost our friend Patricia Strong because we had two lovely ladies who were ready to step forward. Jill Washington joined our church about a year after Patricia first came. Jill had been attending a circle that Patricia hosted in her own home but after some time she moved the circle to St. Brigid's. This then became our advanced circle, which was together for many years. During this time Jill made the decision to become a spiritualist minister, which she successfully achieved. Kim Degner Taylor was another lovely lady that we were blessed to have as a church member who was developing her skills in mediumship and Kim also decided to become a spiritual minister, which she also succeeded in doing.

A month after Patricia left we received another blessing from Spirit in the form of the lovely Bobbi Pineau. I had briefly met Bobbie before as she was a member of the Calgary First Spiritualist Church. On this occasion, Bobbi showed up for our Sunday morning service and asked to chat with me afterwards. I got a great surprise as Bobbi told me she had moved to Edmonton and asked if she could join our church. I of course said yes and welcomed her with open arms. The only way to describe Bobbi is that she is a beautiful and gentle lady with a heart of pure kindness. Bobbi also had, I believe, thirteen years of service to Spirit with her time at the Calgary church. I would also learn that she had experience of serving on the board of the Calgary church and also on the board of the Spiritualist Church of Canada. Throughout her years as a spiritualist and medium she also took many workshops and courses with very experienced teachers both in Calgary and at the Arthur Findlay Collage in Stansted, London, England. Along with all of the great experience that Bobbi brought to our church she also decided to become a spiritualist minister and of course she successfully completed that course and became the fifth minister at our church.

It turned out that Jill, Kim, and Bobbi did a lot of their studies together and Patricia was involved in both Jill's and Kim's ordinations as she had come back to Edmonton to visit at the same time they were being ordained. Bobbi's ordination was to be a little later, but the Covid-19 virus had gained a firm grip on the world and it led to Bobbi being ordained by one of the ministers of the Spiritualist Church of Canada in a virtual ceremony. There was no fanfare or community celebrations for Bobbi, which was sad because, just like Jill and Kim, she so deserved to be celebrated. I am sure Bobbi knows that her fellow ministers and community appreciate and love her very much. So when Patricia was here we had two ministers and when she left there was just myself, but in a really short time we increased to having four wonderful ministers to serve our church and community. This is a great achievement by Jill, Kim, and Bobbi because there is a lot of study involved and at the same time these ladies received their certificates for mediumship and spiritual healing. It is important to understand that in order to become a certified spiritual medium and spiritual healer you have to pass an examination by the Spiritualist Church of Canada. They have a certain standard that the student has to meet in order to receive a certificate. One has to be dedicated and committed to take the time and study to reach the standard of becoming an evidential medium. As a matter of fact, the learning never ends because as you reach each level of achievement there is always another one ahead of you.

We are very fortunate at St. Brigid's to have such wonderful ministers and mediums who have achieved a high standard for the service they provide. We will always strive to have that standard and only give ethical and evidential mediumship. I am very grateful for Spirit bringing these wonderful ladies into my life and St. Brigid's Spiritualist Church. Spirit is amazing and, as I have learned many times, as one door closes another opens.

19

CHAPTER

SPIRITUAL HEALINGS

Over the years, Spirit has allowed me to be part of many healings and I would like to share some of them with you. I have chosen the following ones because to me they are so amazing that they give you a glimpse of the sacred power of Spirit. This one is about a journeyman carpenter who was self-employed and did home renovations. We will call him Michael, and I hired him in August 2007 to install new doors throughout our home. Later that year on Christmas Eve, a friend of mine who is a wonderful medium and also a friend of Michael's called me and asked me to do healing for him because he had been taken to the hospital and had cancer of his blood. She said he had been given a 15 per cent chance of surviving. I said of course I would and I immediately went to my healing room to do this healing. I prepared myself and called on my healing guides to send healing to Michael. Just then I became very warm all over, to the point where I felt like ripping my clothes off. It was so uncomfortable that I actually spoke out loud and asked my guides, *"What is this about?"* My spirit guide answered immediately and told me that when Michael receives the healing, he too would feel this heat. When I finished the healing I immediately called my medium friend and told her what had happened. She then called Michael's wife and told her the story. An important note here is that Michael was an atheist and it was his wife that had requested a spiritual healing, because he had no belief in this and would never have agreed to it. I did the healing on a Friday evening and Michael's wife visited him on the following Saturday morning. She made casual conversation with him for a while and then she just straight out asked him if he had felt it to be very warm on Friday night. He immediately answered yes and said that it was disgustingly hot and very uncomfortable. He asked her how she knew and she told him about the healing she had requested. He did not say much about that and just let it go. Two days later, on Monday, a group of doctors doing their patient rounds had quite a discussion going on as they were attending Michael. They left his room and returned two hours later and they told Michael that they needed to do more tests because by all indications he was cancer free. A few days later Michael was sent home with a clean bill of health.

Six months later my friend called me and asked if I would do another healing for Michael because she said the cancer was back. Because I was fairly new to spiritual healing I thought to myself that I had failed and told my friend so, but she corrected herself and said no, that it was not the same but this time he had brain cancer. She said he had lost his eyesight so he could not see or drive and of course could not work. I did another healing for Michael right away and this time there was no extreme heat felt by me. I forgot about it and about a month later my friend called me and said, guess who I met today. She then told me that she had met Michael at the local supermarket and that he was fully healed from the brain cancer. He was driving and back at work and enjoying life again. These two healings just blew me away but proved to me the awesome power of Spirit.

Selena Hodges is a lovely lady, a wonderful spiritual medium, and I am happy to say a very good friend of mine. She lives in Austin, Texas in the United States. I met her during a time when she and her husband lived in Edmonton, Alberta due to the nature of her husband's business. Selena became a member of our church and one day after service she told me that she had to return to Texas to have some surgery done and she would be back in a few weeks' time. She then asked me if I would do a healing for her and I assured her I would but she left before telling me what she needed the healing for or what type of surgery procedure she was having. Later that evening I connected with Spirit to have the healing done for Selena and I asked my healing guides to send healing to her for whatever she needed. Spirit then proceeded to let me see them working on Selena. I observed two spirit hands working on the inside of her body, although I could not see what they were doing. When they were finished the hands appeared on the top of her tummy near her belly button and they were moving back and forth in a slow motion, and again I could not see what they were doing. I called Selena and told her what I had seen, hoping she could explain it to me. Selena did not offer any insight but said she was seeing her doctor in a couple of days to have X-rays done before her surgery. After her doctor's visit she called me and she was very excited and then told me that she did not require surgery and she was fully healed. She explained that her surgery was to repair a hernia, which explained the spirit hands I saw working inside her body. Her doctor who had performed surgery on her tummy a few years earlier had noticed that the scar from that time which had healed but had left a high ridge was now low and smooth. This explained the rubbing motion I had seen the spirit hands doing. Selena explained that anytime she wore pants they would irritate this scar because it was located where she would fasten and secure them. Needless to say, she was one happy lady. When Selena returned to Edmonton she made a 500 dollar donation to our church. I told her that it was too generous but she insisted that I had saved her a lot of money by her not having to have the surgery. This particular surgery was not covered by her insurance.

A few years later, Selena and her husband returned to their home in Texas but we always kept in touch. On another occasion Selena had her upper back and shoulders badly hurt when she suffered a fall while attending a show in Las Vegas. She called and asked me to send her healing, which I did, and again she received a wonderful healing from Spirit. Her doctors showed her the X-rays taken on the day of her injury and also after Spirit's healing and pointed out that they were different and everything looked normal and she required no further treatment. In February 2021 Selena contacted me again for healing and she was quite upset. She told me that she had taken a nasty fall and done a lot of damage to both knees and her left hand. Her X-rays showed that she had damaged the meniscus in both of her knees and that she also had arthritis in both knees. She had a deep bone bruise in her left hand. After her spiritual healing I asked her to keep me updated on her condition. For the first couple of days there was not much change but then she began to feel better and better every day. About two weeks later I received a text message late one evening asking if I could call her the following day and that she could hardly wait to talk to me. I was excited now as I could tell that something good was happening. It turns out that Selena had been to see her doctor that day and he took new X-rays because they were going to set an appointment for surgery on her knees. When her doctor saw the X-rays he said to her that her knees would last a long time because they were in great shape and that she did not even have any arthritis in her knees. He actually said to her that whatever she was doing to just keep doing it. Selena, being true to who she is, just told her doctor that she received spiritual healing and he just looked at her for a few seconds and then again said, just keep doing whatever it is.

As you can see, these healings that I have shared with you are simply amazing and proof of the sacred and divine power of God our Creator or whatever your understanding of God is. Words cannot convey how honoured, privileged, and grateful I am that Spirit has allowed me to be a part of this beautiful spiritual healing team. I want to make it very clear that I do not heal anyone, but as a spiritual medium my part in this beautiful process is that I am the connection on Earth that healers in the spirit world need to send the healing rays through and they then continue from me to the person on Earth that they are intended for. That is basically how spiritual healing works and the healing power comes directly from the highest source, which is God, and that is why spiritual healing is recognised as the highest form of mediumship.

Testimonial

Dearest Mr. Lanigan,

I want to take this opportunity to thank you for the many healings you have extended to me. Your gift with Spirit is overwhelmingly amazing!

The first healing came when, after 10 years of intermittent pain with different degrees of severity and many doctors later, I was finally diagnosed with multiple incisional hernias. I called and asked to be placed on your healing list and then found out my aunt had cancer. I went to take care of her the last month of her life and forgot about the pain. I had to go in for a CT scan after returning to home only to discover there was nothing there! I went in to see my surgeon and he was astonished as the scar was different. It had smoothed out and there were no ridges. I did not have to have surgery!

I have had many falls over the last six years causing damage and some requiring surgery. I have been told on more than one occasion, I had arthritis in my knees. In January 2021 I had another serious fall, falling on my right hand, left knee and hitting my face on concrete. I reached out to you for healing. Within a few days I was doing much better and then a month later, I had another fall, calling on you once again. The next day, X-rays showed swelling, nothing broken and I was to see my doctor when I returned home. This is when I found out there was no arthritis, and the meniscus was healed!

I am truly blessed to know you and receive the amazing healings Spirit bestows through you! Thank you so much for the beauty of your heart and soul in the work you are doing for Spirit!

Sincerely,
Selena Hodges

20

CHAPTER

AMAZING REVELATIONS

My favourite spiritual teacher is the wonderful spirit guide Silver Birch and I share his teachings with our congregation at our Sunday morning services. In one of his lessons he tells us that every night as we sleep our Spirit leaves our physical body and returns to the spirit world, where it engages in various activities. It is necessary for us to sleep because our physical bodies need rest to replenish our energy but our spirit does not need to rest, and so instead of just being inactive it leaves and returns to the spirit world where it can be useful. I was always curious as to what I might engage in each night as I returned home to the spirit world. I would get my answer in a most beautiful and innocent way as the following story will show.

Ashley Fry is a lovely young lady who came to my Sunday service sometime in 2011 to check it out. She received a message from Spirit through me that morning which convinced her that communication with our loved ones who have passed on was possible. Ashley became a frequent church member and she took a psychic development course and sat in mediumship development circle and was doing quite well until she had to drop out because she became pregnant with her first child. Her lovely baby boy arrived in due time and she named him Preston. During his first winter, Preston would suffer from congestion in his chest and would be very plugged up which affected his breathing. Ashley was very worried about her baby and she called me and asked me to do healing for him. I of course called on my spiritual healing team and they sent healing to Preston and he recovered quite well. Unfortunately, the following winter Preston became ill with the same conditions. Ashley called me again and my spirit healing team and I did another healing for Preston and he recovered very well and he never got sick like that again. I had not met Preston yet and I would not meet him until he was four years old. It happened one day when I drove my wife to the school where my granddaughter Ceiligh went to as we were to pick her up when school was out. My granddaughter asked me if she could get a Slurpee drink from the local 7-Eleven store, so I drove there to do that. I stayed in my car when we got there because I had a very painful backache. There was parking right opposite my car and who should pull into that spot, but Ashley. She had gone there to buy Preston a Slurpee drink too. My wife and Ashley went into the store together with the children and when they came back out, Ashley pointed me out to Preston and said, "That man is Mommy's friend and his name is Richard." Preston said, "No Mommy, you are wrong because he is the spirit man. I saw him in my dreams when I was a baby and he healed me." Ashley came over to me and told me what Preston had just said to her and it just blew me away. A four-year-old child should not even have the vocabulary to put a sentence like that together but he did and he said it in a manner like he assumed his mother knew this. That one sentence from Preston confirmed to me the teaching from Silver Birch about our spirits returning to the spirit world each night and being involved in service, and as I have been involved in spiritual healings for quite some time now it makes sense that my spirit would be doing healings each night. By the way, the healings that I did for Preston were both done at night time just before I went to bed and baby Preston was fast asleep in his crib in his own home. Whenever I speak about this event I say that this is one of the best messages I have ever received from Spirit and it came through a four-year-old little boy.

Ashley has shared more things that Preston had told her. One time he told her that he didn't like his last mom but he really likes her as his mother this time. He also told her that he would love to go back to the old places because he really likes it there. We can only guess as to where he was talking about. Was this his real home in the spirit world that he was remembering? Another amazing thing that Preston would do was, as he sat in his car seat behind his mum he would have a very intelligent conversation with her about the moon and crescent moons, which he just seemed to know about. All of these amazing revelations from Preston occurred from the time he learned to talk and up to around five years of age and then he began to lose his recollection of such events. Preston is now eleven years of age and he does not speak about any of those events anymore. Why is this? One might ask. The most common belief and the one that makes the most sense is that when a baby is born into our world their spirit comes from the spirit world and for the first few years of its life on Earth its memory of where it came from is still very fresh in its mind. It is recognised that generally by the time they are four to five years old they have become used to their life on Earth and their memories of where they came from fade away. I believe it is important for this to happen otherwise these new spirits would not be able to concentrate on the life they have come back to Earth to live and complete the lessons they wish to learn.

I hope this information encourages all parents to pay close attention to the stories their little ones try to tell them when they are at those early years of life because you may be missing out on a treasure trove of amazing information. By the way, little children do not have imaginary friends. Because it is quite normal for them to see spirit people in those early years because again they have just come from the spirit world and they have retained that spiritual faculty that allows them to see Spirit. This is all very normal to the children and I can only imagine their frustration when they discover that their parents don't believe them and sometimes make a joke about their imaginary friends. My advice to the parents of these children would be to listen to them very carefully and discuss their story with them and try to understand what they are sharing with you. A very important point for parents to remember is that children of that age don't make up stories that are so profound and they just say things exactly the way they see it. That is the beauty of their innocence.

21

CHAPTER

SILVER BIRCH

It would be remiss of me if I did not share some more experiences I was privileged to have with this wonderful spirit guide. On one occasion my friend Sharon Ames called me at around noon and asked me if I could do some healing for her. She said she had a very bad headache and she had to teach a class that evening but she would have to cancel it if her headache did not subside. I was going to be in her area of Edmonton that afternoon so I said yes, I would come and do healing for her. As I got into my car to begin my journey to Sharon I called on my healing guides to draw close to me and we would get prepared for healing and I distinctly saw Silver Birch. I was not prepared for this and I was actually shocked to see him and I quickly asked him what he was doing here. Silver Birch did not answer my question and just faded out of my view. I soon forgot about him and arrived at Sharon's place. I concentrated the healing energy on her head as I placed my hands near her and I walked completely around her to cover all areas. When the healing was finished, Sharon said she felt much better and then she told me that when I came around to the front of her she saw Silver Birch with me. I was stunned but here I had validation from another medium who did not know that I had seen him earlier. For some reason that I do not have the answer for, Silver Birch decided to join in on this healing and also wanted me to know that he did participate in it.

It is very important for me to make crystal clear to the reader that Silver Birch is not my spirit guide and I make no claim to that. I have never figured out why Silver Birch did this so I just remain feeling very blessed by this beautiful experience. Because of this visit from Silver Birch I decided to experiment with our most experienced circle. I called on Silver Birch and asked him if he would visit our circle and make himself known to us. I just told our circle members that I had called on a highly evolved spirit to visit us and that I wanted them to focus on our visitor and see what they came up with and I joined in on this exercise too. What I saw was our circle members sitting around an outdoor fire and Silver Birch standing just behind us as if he was just observing us. Most of our circle members saw the same thing and also felt an incredible amount of love coming to them. We have done this a few times and have always had a beautiful experience.

Over the years I have had the pleasure of meeting some wonderful spiritual teachers who are excellent mediums and hail from England. Many of them have attended and studied at the Arthur Findlay Collage in Stansted, London and some of them now teach there, which is a great achievement as only the very best are accepted for that. I mention this because I learned from them that it is well known at the collage about Silver Birch visiting mediumship development circles all around the world. He takes great interest in the growth of spiritualism and the development of authentic mediums everywhere. It was very assuring for me to hear this from people that I totally respect and trust because it validates to me that Silver Birch is actively doing this. You see, there is a very fine line between connecting with a spirit and having your mind make up something that you want to achieve, and that is the difference between a well-developed medium and someone who is not. Silver Birch has stated that he does not wish to be a spirit guide to one individual ever again but it is very exciting and reassuring to know that he is checking in on us to make sure we are doing well with our development. I am so very grateful for the personal interaction and the beautiful teachings from this wonderful spirit guide. Thank you, Silver Birch.

22

CHAPTER

SPIRIT REVEALS MY MISSION

I am always so pleasantly surprised at how Spirit lays the stepping stones to pave the way for an event to take place. I have personally experienced this many times during my life and I know of other people who have had the same thing happen to them, and so it was with this next amazing spiritual experience. On July 27, 2020 I had a complete knee replacement surgery and this would keep me off work for quite some time. In September I was sitting in my back yard, reading one of the Silver Birch books when I learned something very exciting about spiritual healing. Now, I want to point out that I have read all of the Silver Birch books many times not only for my own knowledge but I regularly use his teachings at our weekly Sunday service and somehow I had missed this wonderful information that I was now reading. This information prompted me to set about writing a spiritual healing program. I was very excited about this and I spent the next few days putting the idea together. It all came together very easily and that is because Spirit gave me the idea and all the information I would need for this program and, as you will see, this was the beginning of something Spirit was setting up.

Before I go any further it is important that I share with you an odd experience that I have had on three occasions during my mediumistic development. The first time it happened I was at a complete loss as to what was going on. I found myself standing in front of a very large brick wall. As I looked up I could not see the top of the wall as it was so very high and as I looked left and right I could not see the end of the wall as it seemed to go on forever. I realised that I could not go over or around it and instinctively I knew I could not go backwards. I was at a standstill and did not know what to do. Then I actually had the feeling that I was done and had nothing left to offer and I told my fellow circle members how I felt and that I would soon be leaving. They were all totally shocked and in disbelief because they knew the passion and commitment I had for Spirit. My good friend and go-to lady, Patricia Strong, was away in Australia when this happened. She came back about ten days later and when I explained to her what I was feeling, she said she fully understood. Patricia then told me that she had the same experience as I did and that I had come to a certain point in my development and Spirit wanted me to decide if I wanted to stay where I was or move ahead with my development. I was so relieved to hear this and immediately declared to Spirit that I totally wanted to move ahead and keep learning. Patricia told me that I would be moving up to a higher vibration and that some changes would be coming to me. She was right, and the first thing I noticed was my taste for some foods changed. White bread, tomatoes, and mandarin oranges just did not taste good anymore and over the years other foods were added to the list. My mediumship also changed immediately for the better. I always got good information but it came very fast and within a couple of minutes the sitter who I would be working with would totally understand the information and recognise the Spirit that I had connected with. As a result of that I would finish up my demonstration in a few minutes. The first time I did a demonstration after this change, Spirit slowed down how I received the information and it took me a good six or seven minutes, but I also learned to get much more information from my connection as well.

At the time I wrote the healing program I was going through my third and most recent spiritual evolvement. I was so excited about the healing but at the same time I again felt as if I was done with it all. It was very confusing because I was feeling depressed and I was not sure if this was because of the Covid-19 pandemic or the fact that my rehabilitation from my knee surgery was not going well and was taking a lot longer than anticipated. My feeling was that I could walk away from it all and forget that I ever was a medium or had anything to do with spiritualism. So I called my friend Patricia Strong, who had since returned to Australia with her family. I had her do a reading for me to see what Spirit had to say. Patricia does a wonderful reading of spiritual mediumship and tarot. She was doing the tarot part of my reading when she suddenly stopped and said that Spirit was telling her that I had to write a healing program. Patricia's reading for me was very evidential but this piece of information was most important to me. I told Patricia that I had just finished writing the program the day before my reading. As I chatted to Patricia after my reading she invited me to participate in a guided healing meditation that she hosted once a week. She reminded me that I was always doing something for others and I never do anything for myself. I agreed to join Patricia's group as I very much enjoy her guided meditations. During the first one that I participated in, I was totally surprised when I was joined by the Spirit I had named The Shining One. Eleven years had passed since I first met that dazzling spirit in my sacred place with my spirit guide. I stayed in the meditation group for nine straight weeks and The Shining One showed up in every meditation. The evening of the ninth meditation was totally amazing and changed my life forever. I don't remember what Patricia named this meditation but we were guided as follows.

Imagine you are walking along a golden sandy beach and you come across a small boat. This boat has lovely cushions and blankets lining the floor and you board the boat and make yourself comfortable by lying down on them. Your spirit guide is with you as the boat begins to leave the shore and heads out to sea. Not long after you set sail you see a small island and realise your boat is heading towards it. Soon your boat docks at the island and you get off and begin to walk along a pathway that leads through the trees. After a short walk you come to a clearing in the forest and there is a nice comfortable armchair waiting for you. You sit down and relax as you wait to be joined by a spirit that is going to teach you a spiritual lesson. You are then left in the quietness to enjoy your spiritual experience and you will be called back after twenty minutes. I followed the guided meditation all the way until we reached the places where the armchair was and then things changed for me. I saw the armchair and as I went to sit down I found myself on the back of a beautiful, pure white stallion. The horse took off and went into the forest and I was dropped off and the horse disappeared. Then I had an odd experience where I felt that I was literally sliding up a tree. This tree seemed like it was a hundred feet tall but it was no problem for me as I could go from the bottom to the top very easily and I felt like I could slide out on the branches to the very tip of them and never fall off. I actually did not like this because I thought I was a snake by how I was experiencing the sliding on the tree. Spirit recognised what I was feeling and began to speak to me. They told me that I was not sliding on the trees but that I was actually blending with them. Spirit then said to me that nature was always true and so are you. They explained it this way to me: They said that a tree will always be a tree, a flower will always be a flower, and even a blade of grass will always be a blade of grass. Spirit was telling me in a very unique way that they knew they could trust in me. Then they said that I came to Earth on a healing mission and that I was being guided by The Shining Ones. Well, that statement just blew me away as it was so direct and clear, there was no misunderstanding the message. In one sentence I understood what spiritual work I would be doing for the remainder of my life and now I knew why

I had seen The Shining Ones so long ago when they introduced themselves to me. I now also understood why Spirit taught me about spiritual healing and allowed me to be part of so many wonderful and amazing healings so far in my life. I feel truly blessed, privileged and honoured to be part of a spiritual healing team and I am very excited for the healing possibilities to come. It is very rewarding to have Spirit specify your life mission to you because I now know beyond a shadow of a doubt what exactly I have to do.

The healing program that Spirit helped me to write has been tested many times over the past six months, with amazing results. After I used this method for about six months I began to realise that when the healing was over it was taking me about two or three minutes to fully come back to normal reality. I did not think much of this but it felt very good and relaxing. I was anxious to know what was coming up for me with the healing mission that Spirit revealed to me so I called my lovely friend Shelley Youell again to have her give me a spiritual assessment. Shelley is a brilliant spiritual medium and she has a wonderful connection to Spirit. Her readings and spiritual assessments are amazingly accurate. Shelley began by telling me that I have just finished writing a whole chapter in my book on spiritual healing which was totally correct. She went on to tell me that my book would be published and that there would be a second book later about spiritual philosophy and teachings. She then told me that I have two new spirit guides assigned to me and both were now part of my healing team. She told me that one of them was here to teach me about understanding emotions and the other guide was an Indigenous man who was a healer and a Shaman when he lived on Earth. She said he has already been helping me with the healings and he also was teaching me trance healing. She went as far as to say that sometime in the future I would do trance healings in public and this guide would speak through me and explain to the audience how the healing was being done. This was a wonderful piece of information as it confirmed to me that I was already going into a slight trance, because this is what I was experiencing at the end of each healing when it would take me two or three minutes to come back to reality. I am so very pleased and grateful that these new guides have been assigned to me and I look forward to learning all I can from them so that I can become an even better instrument in service to Spirit. I have always been interested in trance mediumship and healing because if one can work in trance the quality and strength of the mediumship and healings are far superior. This is because the human being is passed by and the information and the healing power then come directly from Spirit.

It is now the middle of May 2021 and my spiritual life story is up to date. I am excited for what the future holds for me but I do know that the possibilities are endless. I feel ever so privileged and eternally grateful to Spirit for the beautiful life I have lived so far and it has been an honour to share this with you. I sincerely hope that you enjoy this story and that you gain inspiration and some learning about the magnificent and sacred power that is available to everyone. This is Spirit. I tell all my friends that I have the best job in the world and that is being…

In Service to Spirit

Blessings to all,
Richard Lanigan
May 20, 2021

Lightning Source UK Ltd.
Milton Keynes UK
UKHW010057300422
402273UK00001B/380

9 780228 862505